To Love Is To Listen

Transform Your Relationships & Your Life With A Powerful New Way To Listen

Mary Schiller

Copyright © 2016 Mary Schiller

All rights reserved.

www.toloveistolisten.com & www.maryschiller.com

ISBN: 1540648990
ISBN-13: 978-1540648990

DEDICATION

To everyone who wants to listen ... and be heard.

Contents

Acknowledgment	i
Introduction Are You a Good Listener?	1
Chapter 1 How We Typically Listen	5
Chapter 2 Listen Closely	13
Chapter 3 Transformative Listening, Step 1	24
Chapter 4 Transformative Listening, Step 2	36
Chapter 5 Listen, and Be Transformed	43
Chapter 6 Being Heard	53
Chapter 7 We're Talking About Love	58
Chapter 8 Frequently Asked Questions	69
Chapter 9 Share The Love	73

Acknowledgement

To my husband, Jeff, who has always had such patience when listening to me, *thank you*.

Introduction
Are You A Good Listener?

My whole life, I had always thought I was a good listener.

It started when I was a young child, plunking on the keys of the family piano in the living room of our unassuming tract house in Edina, Minnesota. I would sit on the piano bench for hours, my feet dangling in mid-air because I was too small to reach the pedals. I'd play nursery rhymes that my mother would sing to me, or I'd mimic the songs on my records (yes, I'm old enough to have had a record player back then). Since I was just three or four years old at the time, I couldn't read music. All I knew was that I could make music myself by listening to songs and then finding the right keys on the piano.

As I got older, I continued to study the piano, earning my bachelor's degree as a music major at the University of California, Los Angeles. While I don't have perfect pitch, in college I was adept at listening to complex compositions, like operas and symphonies, and then analyzing and explaining what was happening in the music.

When I had my own child, naturally I still saw myself as a good listener. I took to motherhood quite easily. I wasn't one of those moms who had a lot of concerns about my parenting skills, and part of that was because I had confidence in my ability to listen to what my daughter was saying — and to hear what she really needed from me.

Later on, I earned master's degrees in both English and education, and once again, I reaffirmed to myself that I was an excellent listener. I was teaching at a university, helping students to become more proficient writers. In one-to-one tutoring sessions, I would sit with students and listen to them tell me about what they were trying to achieve with their essays, and I would often try to read between the lines of what they wrote and help them in other aspects of their life, too. As young people first striking out on their own, they were often going through a lot of ups and downs. I wanted to be someone that they could come to with problems, someone in whom they could place their trust.

If you had asked me whether I was a good listener, I would have said yes, absolutely. I was attentive. I was adept at giving people solid advice and being sympathetic. Perhaps like you, I also attended various "listening training" sessions in different jobs over the years, which taught me how to be an active listener and mirror back to the other person what they had been saying to me.

So put all of that together, and you had someone — me! — who really thought that listening was one of her best skills.

But I was missing something — something big. I may have been a good listener on the surface, but now I know that there's an entirely different way to listen that literally — not figuratively — changes people's lives, including that of the listener. It has definitely changed mine.

In this book, I'll share with you what has transformed my life, and every relationship in it, for the better. I'll show you how to listen for something that cannot be heard -- something that will give you a beautiful new way to love.

One last thing before we begin. Take your time in reading this book. It may be short, but there's a lot packed into these few pages — and a lot that will be brand new to you. Give yourself the space to take it all in.

Chapter 1
How We Typically Listen

You know how to listen, right? Maybe, like me, you've always thought of yourself as a good listener.

In this chapter, we'll explore what happens during a typical conversation. You may be surprised at what we uncover.

As an experiment, pay attention the next time you talk to someone, whether it's an "important conversation" or not, and see if you notice what's really happening alongside, beneath and around the conversation.

Listening for Information

When we listen to someone, generally we start by paying close attention to the details. We're taking in what the person says, and immediately, we're trying to figure things out and make sense of what we're hearing.

We might compare what they're saying to our own ideas or to other things we've read or seen. If we've talked with the person before, we may start recalling conversations we've had with them in the past. As we listen for information, our brains are working overtime, like a whirring, super-high-speed computer processor.

For example, you may be having a drink one evening with a friend who is telling you that she's having major trouble with her boss. This "horrible boss," as your friend describes her, is overly demanding and short on giving raises that are long overdue. While your friend is talking, you may be hearing thoughts in your head like, "She's mentioned this situation before. What has she said? Did she already go to her boss' boss or to Human Resources to ask for support? Does this relate to anything in my own work experience?"

Engaging Our Other Senses

Not only are we using our ears, but we're also using our eyes, looking — often subconsciously — for certain signs in someone's body language to see if they are telling the truth. Do they seem nervous? Are they potentially lying to us?

With your friend, you may be watching for subtle, or not so subtle, cues that show you she's truly distressed. You might be looking for tears or signs of anger, like clenched fists, although you're not doing all of this consciously.

Deciding What to Say Next

And of course, while you're processing all the information your friend is sharing and noticing her body language, you're also mentally compiling a potential response: "What could I say that's helpful to her? Should I tell her to forget about it and find another job, or should I tell her to go talk to someone in Human Resources — or maybe a counselor or even a lawyer? I want to be sure and say the right thing and not upset her."

Much of the time we spend listening is actually spent trying to figure out what we're going to say next. When you're on the receiving end of this kind of listening, it's easy to tell when someone is no longer listening to you and, instead, is in their own head just waiting to blurt something out.

For instance, I used to work for a boss who had a habit of listening to the first half of someone's sentence and then interrupting the person before they could finish (more on this situation in a later chapter). The results, as you might imagine, were misunderstandings, loss of rapport and respect, and a whole host of other problems in our workplace.

Disagreeing with Someone

If we're listening to someone with whom we have a disagreement, then everything in our heads takes on a completely different tone. Immediately, sometimes before they've said anything at all, we're looking for holes in their argument. Instead of listening, we're calculating when we're going to say something, what we're going to say and how we'll say it to best make our own case. In those situations, our ability to really hear the other person, even on a surface level for information, is pretty poor. Is it any wonder why people rarely come to a consensus under these circumstances?

Thanks in large part to learning a new way of listening that is the subject of this book, my husband and I rarely argue anymore. But when we used to have a disagreement in years past, I am positive — as embarrassing as this is to admit — that I never really heard anything he said. My mind was too busy defending my side of the argument and waiting to pounce on any errant fact he might utter.

For instance, if we were discussing how to more equitably divide our household responsibilities, my mind would immediately be filled with defensive thoughts: "He can say whatever he wants, but I do the bulk of the work around here. How dare he question me!" And I listened to every one of these thoughts, believing that they were actually going to help me win the argument. Can you relate?

Listening for Validation

Someone might be talking about a topic that we're interested in, and we're listening for points that validate our perspective or our opinion on that topic. In that case, we'll automatically pick out particular phrases that they're saying that support our point of view and ignore everything else. Politics come to mind as an example of this type of listening, where we often listen only for statements and facts that at least *appear* (where they actually do or not doesn't seem to matter) to confirm our current opinions.

Or let's say I ask you to look for red cars on the road. Suddenly, that's all you see: red cars are everywhere! It's the same thing when we have an idea or opinion that we want reinforced. We'll tune out everything that doesn't support it, even if there are valid reasons why we should listen to other points of view.

Acting and Reacting

Taking a look at this breakdown of what's going on when we're listening to someone reveals a lot, doesn't it? It shows us that we may be listening, but there's plenty of activity happening in the process of listening.

The thing is, we've either been told outright that this is the best way to listen, or we simply don't know any other way to listen: we're listening for information; we're observing the person's body language; we're trying to figure out what to say; we're waiting for the other person to make a mistake; we're listening for validation; and on the off chance we actually want to help someone, it usually comes in the form of giving them advice or simply nodding or saying, "I understand." We are taking in what the person is saying, yes, but we're also reacting to it, and then we're acting upon what we hear — or what we think we hear through all the noise.

Listening Differently

After going through this description of listening in this chapter, I'm sure you can see that even if you're not the one doing the talking, there's a lot going on when you're in a conversation with someone.

But this new way of listening, which we'll talk about next, truly is transformational, for both you and the other person. And it's like nothing you've heard before (wink, wink!).

Before we venture on, I'd like you to take a moment to write about the relationship(s) in your life that you wish were better. It could be with anyone from a colleague to a spouse, a child or friend — anyone at all. Next to each one, write out what might happen if that relationship could be better. What are your dreams for how things could be between you? I'll leave some space here for you to write a response.

What You Heard in This Chapter

- Listening, in the traditional sense, is more reactionary than anything else.
- We're typically listening for information, watching someone's body language, trying to figure out what to say next, and often looking for validation of our own ideas and trying to poke holes in what the other person is saying.
- When we stop to examine how we're listening, we may wonder if we're hearing anything at all.

Chapter 2
Listen Closely

So far, we've looked at listening in the traditional sense: what some people might call "active listening."

I'd like to ask you another question, so let's pause for a moment here.

Think about a recent conversation that didn't go the way you wanted it to. Perhaps you intended to point something out to the other person to help them, or to help your relationship with them, and things spiraled into an argument. Or maybe you didn't feel like you got your message across effectively — they didn't really hear you.

Can you see something you did in terms of listening (or not listening) that might have contributed to the conversation going astray? Write out your answer here or on a separate piece of paper.

Are you ready to hear — pun intended — about a new way to listen? Great! Then let's get right into it.

Set Aside What You Know

At this point in the book, I'd like you to try to forget everything I just said about the typical way of listening and what it means to be a "good listener." And please try to forget everything you thought you knew about listening before you picked up this book.

We're starting with a clean slate, as if you know nothing at all about how to listen to someone. Pause and take a deep breath along with me.

(I don't do that often enough, do you? New Year's Resolution: Take more deep breaths.)

I'm about to tell you something that you may not believe, but here goes. The way of listening that we're all accustomed to is *rubbish*, especially when it comes to having effortlessly successful relationships with people. It might be fine if you're trying to understand facts and figures — intellectual stuff. But with people? It's absolutely useless.

And worse than being useless, although the typical way to listen to others is purporting to give you the kinds of relationships you want, it's actually keeping you from having them. You want relationships with your friends, colleagues, acquaintances and family that are fulfilling, easy, fun, loving, close, connected — right?

Traditional listening won't help you. Not one bit. Even when we parrot back to the person what we heard them say — sometimes using those words, "This is what I heard you say" — it's still engaging our brain in a way that's not helpful, particularly in relationships. So …

If we're not listening to the words someone is saying and trying to put it all together and make sense of it; and if we are not listening to someone in order to respond to them in a reactionary way, either for their benefit or ours, then how else can we listen to them?

You've Already Experienced It

What's really wonderful is that you actually already know all about what I'm calling "transformative listening." You, yourself, have engaged in it, even though you may not have been doing so consciously. I'm positive that you've had the experience of listening to someone where their words started to fade into the background — and I don't mean because you're actually trying to tune them out and float into a daydream. We've all been in that situation, like when we've been listening to a boring teacher (I'm remembering my college economics class right about now).

No, I'm talking instead about tuning out the words someone is saying and tuning in to something else — something happening beneath their words. To give you an idea of what I mean, I'd like to tell you a brief story.

An Unforgettable Conversation

When I was teaching writing at a university in California several years ago, I was working mostly with freshmen. It was near the end of the academic term, close to finals week. One of the nicest students in my class, who had been doing fine and was a solid writer, didn't show up for a private writing conference with me. He hadn't been to class for two or three sessions before then, either, so I was a little concerned about him, wondering if something had happened.

A few days after he missed that appointment with me, I was in my office during my regular weekly open office hours, and he knocked on the door, which was ajar. He stepped inside and asked if he could talk to me, and I said, "Of course. It's nice to see you."

I could sense right away that something was wrong. His eyes were downcast, and he looked like he hadn't eaten much since I'd seen him last — his clothes were hanging off of him, and his cheeks were sunken in.

He said to me, "I'm so sorry I had to miss our appointment, and I'm really sorry that I haven't been to class, but something happened in my family. It's been hard for me to keep up with my work these past couple of weeks."

Without consciously thinking about it, I found myself tuning out the words he was saying and listening to him in a different way. I remember the sensation vividly because it was like everything around us — the bookshelves, my desk, the windows that looked out on the sunny California campus — faded into the background, and I began to feel a strong connection to him on a human-to-human level.

At the moment when I felt that connection most powerfully, he was telling me that his younger brother had committed suicide, apparently on his sixteenth birthday. They had found his brother's body a few days later in a cement water main pipe near his parents' property.

I spent the next few minutes listening to him but not really hearing the words he was saying. I felt like I was listening to the deepest part of this young man's heart. Not only that, I felt like I knew — I absolutely knew, without a doubt — that he was going to be OK.

Actually, it wasn't that I knew he was *going* to be OK. I knew *he already was OK*, right then and there, despite his suffering and despite the situation he was in.

After telling me about his brother, he said to me, through tears, "Ms. Schiller, I can get all my work turned in before the end of the quarter. I know it's coming up soon, but I can do it. I don't need or want an extension."

I assured him that he could have an extension if he needed it, but he was adamant that he didn't need any special treatment. When he was done talking, he turned to leave … and collapsed into my arms, sobbing. I helped him find his way to the student health center on campus. By the time we arrived there, he was fully upright and walking with a sense of purpose. Without knowing what, exactly, had happened, I knew he had found himself again — and that that "self" was strong, healthy and resilient.

Can you recall at least one time in your life when you have listened to someone in that way, from a place of really being connected to the other person, of seeing through the words and into the person themselves?

An Everyday Example

Transformative listening doesn't have to be quite so dramatic every time (thank goodness). For instance, have you ever listened to a young child who is crying and telling you they lost their favorite toy or that a friend didn't invite them to a birthday party? When you listen, you can see through the child's tears, and you can comfort them freely because you know they're really all right, despite their emotions.

There is no permanent damage done to the child because they lost a toy or didn't get to go to a party. They might be upset for a while, but that momentary "upset-ness" doesn't mean that there's something wrong with them on a deeper level. You see through the story, and you experience the child for who he or she truly is: unbroken and unharmed.

That's the kind of listening that I'm talking about in this book: a way to listen from that secure and knowing place within you more often and almost automatically, so those powerful emotional connections are a more routine part of your life experience.

Not only that, as you'll see in a later chapter, you can listen to someone tell you something as tragic as my student losing his brother to suicide, and you can know without doubt that they are all right — despite the situation or their suffering.

Let's pause and reflect. Imagine for just a moment if everyone on earth listened to others this way. What might happen if people really heard one another — listening past the story and the circumstances, and into one another's inner strength and resilience? How might the world change? Write out a few ideas here or on another piece of paper.

That conversation with my student happened a dozen years ago as I'm writing this book. But I still remember it, and I still remember the feeling of connection to someone I barely knew. Back then, I didn't know what I was really doing as a listener in that situation. Now, I do — and this understanding has made all the difference.

I'd like you to recall a time when you listened to someone in that way. Remember how it felt for you, and imagine how it might have been for the other person.

Conversely, perhaps you can think of a time when someone listened to you like this and how it felt to be heard — really heard — for who you are, as opposed to what someone thought you were. For instance, is there someone in your life who forms an easy connection with you when you talk with them? Write out your impressions here or separately.

So where does this kind of listening — "transformative listening" — come from? What are we tapping into when we listen to another human being in this way, and why might it be really helpful to be able to listen from that place of connection more often? That's what we'll be discussing next.

What You Heard in This Chapter

- The typical way we listen to people is not particularly helpful in our relationships.
- You have already experienced transformative listening, either as the listener or the person being listened to.
- Transformative listening is about understanding who the other person truly is: a whole and unbroken human being, no matter what they may be saying to you, what their situation might be or what kind of emotional experience they're having in that moment.

Chapter 3
Transformative Listening, Step 1

When you're on the receiving end of someone listening to you in the way I described with my student in the previous chapter, it can be an amazing and liberating experience.

You might have the sense of being enfolded in the other person's presence: a feeling of non-judgment, safety and security. You may also notice your own resilience rising to the surface without any effort whatsoever.

But you may also agree with me that this kind of encounter is quite rare. That's why I've written this book: to help you engage in transformative listening with others and, in turn, allow them to have that experience of truly being heard and finding their own inner strength without any effort whatsoever.

As you'll soon discover, transformative listening has incredible benefits not just for the person being listened to, but also for you as the listener.

In this chapter, we'll explore step 1 in the transformative listening process: recognizing that we are not the stories we hear inside our own heads.

We've already talked about the fact that typically, people are listening for information, for a chance to talk again, or for an opportunity to share advice or their opinion. Even when we attend trainings about listening, what we're learning is still based on that kind of information-based listening experience.

Transformative listening, on the other hand, is both natural but also needs to be learned — or, rather, the other type of listening needs to be "unlearned." That's what we'll delve into in this chapter and the next, because when we're engaged in transformative listening, we're listening from someplace other than our intellect, other than our own thoughts, other than what we typically see as our "self."

That bears repeating, so you may want to take another look.

When we listen in this transformative way, we're listening from a different place within ourselves, which means that we need to answer a couple of key questions.

Where is this place? *What* is this place?

Let's find out by starting from the top … of your head.

That Voice You're Hearing In Your Head? It's Not You

Before we can talk in depth about transformative listening, we need to look in a direction that may be a little — or maybe more than a little — surprising to you.

I walked through my entire adult life, until I was in my early 50s, with a misunderstanding that I'm betting you're living with, too. To put it simply, I didn't understand that the voice in my head (the one that you have, too) wasn't really *me*.

Can I just say what a relief that is? Because I have to tell you, sometimes that voice says really weird stuff. Does yours?

For example, for nearly thirty years, that voice inside my head told me I had to be anxious and afraid most of the time; it also told me that I had a mental illness called post-traumatic stress disorder. And it wasn't just the voice in my head that told me that. It was lots of professionals, too. They said I had gone through such a traumatic experience — a violent first marriage — that I would always have PTSD.

But a couple of years ago, someone kindly pointed out to me that perhaps that wasn't actually true — that instead, if I was experiencing that horribly stressed-out feeling, it was coming from a momentary thought, and nothing more.

In other words, my feelings and my experience were comprised of fleeting, transient thoughts that had nothing to do with me or my past. I had simply been listening to these thoughts and believing that they had great significance — as if they really made up who I was, as a person.

I learned that I didn't have any control over these thoughts, but that was OK. I'd spent years trying to change them and couldn't. Instead, I had the option to not listen to them anymore. They could come into my mind, but I could ignore them and do nothing.

I remember thinking to myself, "Is is really that simple?" I was skeptical, to say the least. So I decided to test it.

I'd hear one of those familiar, anxious thoughts, and I'd ask myself, "Do I really need to listen to that thought and do what it says? Or is this constant chatter of thinking more like noise or static — and there's actually beautiful music, or perhaps a luxurious stillness, waiting for me underneath it somewhere that I just can't hear right now?"

For a while, every time those stress-related thoughts would come into my mind, I would simply sit with them and not react. It didn't feel great, but over a short time, the anxiety started to subside, and those kinds of thoughts came to mind less often.

And then, I saw something rather basic but that wasn't obvious to me before: if I could *listen* to the voice in my head, then I could not possibly *be* the voice in my head. In other words, I have thoughts and you have thoughts. But those thoughts aren't me or even mine, really. The thoughts that go through your mind aren't you. We have eyes and noses and hands, but those aren't who we are. What are these thoughts, then? What are they really doing?

A Convincing Illusion

Thoughts create what we see in front of us as our reality, but it doesn't mean it's all *true*. No matter how it may look to us, everything we're experiencing — our feelings and how we see things — is coming from the thoughts rattling around inside our mind that we happen to be paying attention to and taking seriously right then.

Nothing we experience, nothing we feel, is ever coming from "out there." It's always coming from "in here."

How do we know? Because feelings can't be transmitted *from* something and *into* us. It's not physically possible, for example, for a traffic jam to somehow send stress into our bodies. Only thoughts can do that. You can test this yourself by noticing, for instance, that sometimes you're bothered when you're sitting in traffic, and other times, you're not.

The illusion that thoughts create for us in our daily experience is incredibly powerful. Thought, as a whole, does a good job of trying to convince us that everything we hear in our heads is true. But the fact is, we're listening to a story, and while it looks real, it isn't. Because *we are not our thinking*. We are not the stories we tell ourselves. Even when the story looks very, very real to us, it's still made up.

Thoughts — particularly if they have wound-up, stressed-out feelings attached to them — aren't worth listening to much of the time. Often, they're not telling us anything particularly useful, so why would we want to reinforce them? We can simply let them float on by and not worry about them at all.

As an example of what can happen when we ignore our thinking, I recently had a conversation with a client who was convinced that they weren't "good enough" to pursue a creative endeavor. They said that they felt this way forever because of the way they were raised. They were distressed by these thoughts and feelings, but as I listened to my client describe what they were going through, I didn't ask many questions or venture too far into the details — because clearly, it was a made-up story inside their head that they had been listening to for their entire life.

They believed that that *story* was actually who they *were*.

During the conversation, I didn't try to sympathize, nor was I even feeling concerned about the person. I knew they were perfectly whole and healthy; it's just that they were listening to some old, familiar thoughts and believed that they were true.

As our conversation progressed and I continued to listen in this transformative way, my client's voice started to slow down, and I could hear that they were beginning to let go of that story without any effort whatsoever. They stopped listening to those old thoughts and begin to experience something else — something really powerful.

What happened afterward was astonishing to me.

Within just a few hours of finishing our conversation, my client had produced a piece of art that had been held dormant inside them for years. Any fearful thoughts or "I'm not good enough" thoughts had faded into the background, and the inner and infinite well of creativity had risen to the surface within them — allowing for effortless inspiration and artistry.

My client wasn't that story they had been listening to for their entire life, of course, but so much more.

What is Real?

Right about now, you may be saying, "Wait a minute, Mary. Are you telling me that our thoughts paint a picture or tell a story that looks real to us, but we shouldn't believe it? Sort of like a mirage? If that's the case, then what is real? I want to hear an answer to that!"

The answer to that question is actually quite simple. I'll use myself as an illustration. I used to have a lot of thoughts like these:

"What's wrong with you, Mary? Why can't you stop feeling so anxious all the time?"

"You're never going to feel at peace because of what you've been through in life. Face it: you're broken and unfixable."

"No one ever recovers from PTSD. Just learn to cope and move on."

When I stopped giving those thoughts any attention, something incredible happened. I began to experience what seemed like the real version of *me*.

It was the *me* I had been searching for all my life, that I had been told had been swallowed up by trauma and PTSD, never to return. She hadn't been destroyed, after all.

At first, I had no inkling that when I stopped taking my thoughts so seriously, what would emerge was a feeling of inner spaciousness and peace, which is what I had wanted so desperately my whole life. I had searched everywhere for that feeling, not realizing that it wasn't just within me, but it *was* me.

Dropping down into that beautiful space within — the space that allows us to truly hear another person — happens to each of us the moment we see the role of our thoughts. They're giving us this amazing "human being experience," our emotions and feelings, but they are not who we really are.

What's real is what's beneath the stories we tell ourselves, what's beneath all of the thoughts we have and their accompanying feelings.

If we're on the receiving end of a conversation where someone is telling us a story, the way to sink into this transformative listening space is to see that story for what it is: a reflection only of their thinking in that moment and that moment only, and not of who they really are. A person can't be defined or contained by momentary thinking.

That's the simple step 1 of transformative listening: look beyond your own thinking, because it isn't who you are, and typically it's not telling you anything useful — particularly when it gets you feeling tied up in knots. Don't do anything about those thoughts. Don't analyze them or try to pin them down. Wait them out, and they will pass on by. And in that moment, the feeling of *you* will emerge.

Wouldn't you like to be someone who can help another person change their life? I thought so. Let's keep going deeper in step 2, next, and see what we uncover.

What You Heard in This Chapter

- Step 1 of transformative listening is recognizing that you are not the voice in your head. Those thoughts generate your feelings, but they aren't who you are.

- What's real and true is what lies beneath those stories that run through our heads all day long.
- We are allowed to ignore out thinking and listen from a quieter space within ourselves.

CHAPTER 4
TRANSFORMATIVE LISTENING, STEP 2

In the last chapter, we uncovered something truly amazing: we are not our thoughts. The thoughts that go through our minds create the experience we're having — our feelings — but they're not who we are.

Not only that, we don't have to worry about that voice in our head that's chattering away all day long. We can't predict what these thoughts will be, nor can we change them. So why pay them much attention at all? Over time and after lots of experimenting with simply leaving my thoughts and feelings alone and not worrying about them, I saw that I cannot be contained or controlled by what thoughts I happen to have.

And neither can you.

There's an "I" that is part of something larger than what I see when I look in the mirror. If I imagine that I'm looking at myself from the outside using a camera, I can zoom out, and zoom out, and zoom out, and I can see you, and me, and everyone on Earth as part of something much bigger than could ever be confined to a thought or to a string of thoughts.

Understanding this for yourself will allow you to listen to another person in a deeper, more impactful way than you may have ever believed possible. And it can change the other person's life — and yours. Let's look at step 2 of transformative listening and see where we find ourselves.

The "Overview Effect"

A friend recently reminded me of the experience that astronauts have when they see Earth from space, what's called the "overview effect." From that vantage point, an astronaut has a shift in consciousness about the supposed divisions and conflict that separate us from one another. Instead, Earth and its inhabitants appear as one: a precious ball suspended in the universe that must be nourished, cherished and protected.

This "overview effect" is not limited to astronauts. We can experience it, too — every time we engage with another human being through transformative listening.

We see and hear ourselves in them, and we see all of us for who we really are: human beings to be nourished, cherished and protected.

We can connect to another person from this place — or from this space, if we imagine ourselves like the astronauts. But this space I'm referring to isn't among the stars; it's within each of us. That luxurious stillness that is our natural state as human beings, free from the noise of that voice in our heads. A place within us that allows us to hear people, and ourselves, in a different way.

Let's explore this idea a bit further.

Here or on another piece of paper, write about what you've understood so far about your thoughts actually not being who you are. Does this seem real to you, or even possible? If you're not your thoughts, who are you?

I'll leave some space here for you to write your ideas.

What's Beyond the Story

Zoom the camera out again and see where you actually are: not inside a ball of tangled old thoughts or circumstances from which you can't escape, but suspended, like Earth, within an infinite internal universe without any limitations at all.

That's what we can tap into when we engage in transformative listening. We see other people (and ourselves) not as their thinking describes them — with hardships and limitations — but instead as complete human beings with every creative resource they could ever need.

Even if it's tempting to do so, it's much more helpful to someone to *not* engage in the story itself and thereby reinforce it, because that's immaterial. That story has nothing to do with them, and even if it looks true, it isn't; they are the human being beyond and beneath that thought-created story. It's not that you shouldn't be somewhat sympathetic to what the other person is feeling and experiencing. Their feelings are real, just as yours are. It's fine to acknowledge that they are upset or angry or whatever the case may be.

But know this: those feelings are coming from their momentary thoughts, and not from circumstances or anything "out there."

So when we are with someone and we really want to hear them, how can we drop down from our noisy, personal thinking and into this calm, transformational space?

It's not as difficult as you might imagine. Let's start with a question. What have you heard someone say about themselves that hasn't seemed the least bit true to you?

For example, I have a friend who is insecure about his professional capabilities. But every time I talk with him, he shares stories of the latest articles he has read, people he has spoken to and knowledge he has gained — and he clearly knows what he's talking about. What (usually negative) story does someone in your life believe about themselves: something that you know is completely unfounded? Do you think if I asked that person the same question about you, that they would have an answer? Write out your ideas here or separately.

This is the simple step 2 of transformative listening: Listen past the other person's momentary thinking, past the story they're telling you, and hear who they really are.

In other words, listen for what it is inaudible.

When you are listening from this naturally understanding and non-judgmental space inside yourself, you are listening to that infinite human being across from you, and not to the momentary thinking that happens to be going on inside their minds right then.

This act is so powerful because without engaging in the other person's thought-created reality, without jumping into and agreeing with their story, you can connect to them on the deepest level possible. That's where, and how, transformation takes place. And it's effortless.

We'll talk more about transformation, and I'll share an intensely personal example of it, in the next chapter.

What You Heard in This Chapter

- We don't have to worry about, or do anything about, our thinking because we are much bigger than what any single string of thoughts could possibly tell us about we are.
- Step 2 of transformative listening simply involves listening past the other person's story, past their thinking, and connecting to who they really are.
- It's much more helpful to the other person to listen to what's beneath their story instead of engaging with their thinking, which is more than likely not telling them anything that's true.

CHAPTER 5
LISTEN, AND BE TRANSFORMED

Even when life looks chaotic and confusing, when your feelings are taking you to the depths of sadness or despair, underneath all of that is a naturally calm and peaceful *you*.

For most of my life, I didn't know that that was the case. When I was listening to all that anxious, stressed-out thinking that I mentioned earlier, I believed that I was an anxious and stressed-out person. It didn't seem normal to me to be calm; in fact, it seemed just the opposite.

But when I saw that I was not my thinking, and that I didn't even have to listen to those thoughts, I started to experience my natural state of well-being more and more of the time. My mind quieted down all on its own, as it's designed to do, and I began to see my life and other people much more clearly and calmly. It was amazing how quickly this happened, too.

A Powerful Listening Agent

You have this same infinite resilience and clarity available to you: it's what you're made of. As a result, you are a powerful listening agent that can connect deeply with any person you encounter.

It's the real *you* I'm talking about: without an agenda, ulterior motive or goals for a conversation other than simply spending more time in the wide-open space that's already within you — and meeting the other person there.

When we're listening in the more typical way that I described in the first chapter, we're not really listening to the other person. We're listening to our own thinking. Our brain gets fired up, and that voice we're hearing isn't the other person's, but the one jabbering inside our own head. We're caught up in that whitewater stream of thoughts instead of realizing that there's a crystal-clear, peaceful lake just underneath it.

But when we connect to another human being through transformative listening — listening *from* our innate well-being instead of to the voice in our head, and listening *to* the other person's innate well-being instead of to the story they're telling themselves — it can be transformative not just for the person being listened to, but also for us as the listener.

Engaging in Transformative Listening

Transformative listening has two simple steps, which we've been exploring so far in this book.

First, it's recognizing that we can tune out our own thinking (the story that's not really who we are) and listen from the place of natural clarity within ourselves.

And second, it's looking at the other person and seeing past their thinking, too: past the story they're telling you and into who they really are beneath and beyond that story.

The truth is, we are always living in this state of clarity and openness. That's a 24/7 proposition. We're always there; it's not someplace that we need to seek or find. The only reason we don't feel it all the time is because we're human beings, and sometimes we get caught up in our stories: the stories that thoughts are telling us that seem so compelling and real. That's just a function of being human. It's nothing to worry about, nor do you need to do anything to try to change it (and please, don't try to change or manipulate your thoughts — that's impossible, anyway).

When we can simply ignore those thoughts as we listen to another person, the effect is almost like having x-ray vision — as if we can see through the veil of their personal thinking, through the story that they're sharing with us. We can still hear the details of that story, so we can connect with them occasionally on those details, but what we're really seeing and hearing is their true *self* underneath that story.

At the same time, while we're listening to the other person in this way, we're feeling more connected to *our* true selves, too. It's a beautiful symbiotic relationship, where you can feel this wholeness within yourself, and you can also feel it within the other person.

And the effect on me, I can tell you, is an incredible sense of both peace and wide-open space — as if I'm able to take in more and more of the other person who is talking to me, and I mean that in the purest way possible. I have the sensation that all of the miraculous aspects of the human being across from me are being partially absorbed by me, and there is a oneness that emerges between us that is difficult to put into words.

I find it personally transformative whenever I am able to create that kind of connection with someone else. I am looking deeper into myself. I'm looking further in the direction of my own innate well-being as well as the other person's. And it truly is a wonderful feeling — even when the other person might be having a moment where they're experiencing an emotion that's challenging for them. This feeling of peace is still there underneath it all, because it's always there.

When you look past someone's emotions to who they really are, you can see and experience that peace in both of you, no matter what the emotional waves may be. Often when I'm listening to someone in this way, I have the sense that we're both floating in a tranquil sea. So while I don't want to say it's selfish to create this kind of listening experience, it certainly feels refreshing for the person who is doing the listening.

"My Daughter Might Die"

The most poignant example from my own life so far that illustrates transformative listening occurred in spring 2016.

At that time, my daughter — who is in her late 20s as I'm writing this book — was living with my husband and me in New York City while doing her doctoral research. She had also been having some health problems, so we had been a support system to her so that she could focus on what she needed to do to complete her fieldwork for her degree.

One night, my husband and I had gone out to meet a friend for dinner. Before we even made it to the subway station, my husband's cell phone rang. It was our daughter, and she sounded terrified and frantic, saying that she needed to go to the emergency room.

We rushed back home, and sure enough, she was exhibiting a physical symptom that can indicate something deadly is about to happen. As quickly as we could, we all went back to the subway, which was faster than waiting for a taxi or car service in our neighborhood, and made the short trip to the hospital.

I remember as we were walking to the emergency room from the train, I had the thought of, "People's children die sometimes. My daughter might die."

When we arrived and the nurse saw her symptom, she took our daughter inside immediately. Shortly afterward, our daughter was examined by a doctor, who said, with a serious tone to his voice, "Well, it could be nothing. Or it could be something." And by "something," he didn't mean something good, unfortunately.

A few minutes later, my daughter and I were outside the radiology department, waiting for her turn to get a CT scan. What happened next is difficult to describe, but I'll do my best to capture it.

As we waited, we had the most amazing conversation we've ever had.

Both of us were scared — it would only be natural to have fearful thinking right then — but at the same time, we were at peace. She was crying silently, but she told me how much it meant to her that I was there with her right then, and how she knew that I had always been by her side throughout her life.

I shared the same sentiment with her, saying that I appreciated what a support she had been to me, even when she didn't know it. We smiled at memories of going to Disneyland together over the years, of hanging out at the beach, of enjoying our life as a family.

At some point, the dim hallway lights and hospital smell faded into the background, and something else came into the foreground. I noticed that I wasn't listening to my own scary thoughts anymore, nor was I listening to what my daughter was saying so much as listening to *her*. It was as if the two of us were no longer mother and daughter or even two people with bodies anymore.

I was aware of being in this human form in the most unimportant way possible, and instead, I experienced being part of something formless and vast — like those astronauts experiencing the "overview effect."

We were two beings held in the embrace of time and space, while holding onto each other in the physical world.

"It's always been you and me, Mommy," she said, so softly that I wasn't sure it was audible or whether I was hearing it inside my own heart. A female patient on a gurney next to us — the only other person in the waiting area — seemed to notice something, too. She turned to us and said, "That's beautiful."

This conversation changed the way I experience my daily life, so much so that I rarely feel stressed at all anymore. No matter what is happening, no matter what my circumstances are, I sense a deep and calming presence within me that never falters, never seems distant.

Have you ever had an experience where you felt calm and composed, and perhaps connected to another person in this way, even though you were afraid? Write out a few sentences about it.

What You Heard in This Chapter

- Transformative listening isn't just about the person being listened to. When we listen to someone in this way, we can have life-changing transformations, ourselves.

- Listening from that quiet space inside ourselves can create an amazing sense of peace and calm, no matter what might be happening in our circumstances.

- We can be aware of the amazing co-existence of both our human selves and what lies beyond this human experience by engaging in transformative listening.

CHAPTER 6
BEING HEARD

In the previous chapter, I shared my experience of listening to my daughter in the hospital and how affected I was by what came over me: the deepest sense of peace I could imagine, despite the chaotic and fearful thinking I was experiencing at the same time.

What is the effect of this kind of listening on the person who's being listened to? Let's look at what it's like to be on the receiving end when someone is listening to us in this way.

Experiencing Our True Selves

If you have been listened to in this way before, you probably know what that experience is like. As I alluded to earlier, it feels secure as well as liberating. And even if you can sense that the person isn't engaging in your story, there's almost a comfort factor in that, because you know that they are seeing through your story to who you truly are.

When someone listens to me from this space and they're not saying much, I've noticed that very quickly, the story I'm caught up in tends to fizzle out. It trails off into nothingness because suddenly, even if I'm not consciously aware of it, it starts to look less formidable to me, less real to me.

That story that's gotten me so worked up begins to look more like what it is: momentary thinking, and nothing more.

I've had the experience of feeling incredibly relaxed and composed within a short span of time when someone is listening to me in this way.

For example, I was on the phone with a coach a while back, and I had just lost my job. Since I was the sole breadwinner at the time, had no prospects for work and almost no savings, things looked grim to me. I was freaked out and scared, and my world seemed to be crumbling around me. Let's just say that it wasn't the most enjoyable experience I've ever had.

I was telling my coach about what had happened with my job, and I started to notice such a feeling of peace emerging in the midst of the conversation. Very quickly, my anxiety began to subside. Even the speed at which I was talking started to slow down; it was like my foot was coming off the accelerator of a car, and I could feel myself stabilizing.

I sensed that the coach cared not so much about the circumstances that I was talking about, but about *me*. She saw through my story and into the real *me*. All without saying more than a few words.

It was a true gift to have that conversation right then. I remember having the sensation that no matter what feelings I might've been experiencing, even if I was stressed, anxious or terrified, in those few moments the power of that person's transformative presence allowed me to settle down.

The conversation itself, led by someone listening from that wide-open, nonjudgmental space within them, was bringing me back to my own well-being.

What happened to me after the conversation was remarkable, too. Within just a few minutes, I was able to see a clear next step to take after losing my job when, just moments before, my world looked like it had just crashed down on me.

Well-Being Connects to Well-Being

In simple terms, it's really that one person's story/thinking doesn't connect very well to another person's story/thinking, but one person's well-being connects easily to another person's well-being. Our innate well-being acts almost like a magnet. It's always trying to draw us back to it. And when we have someone across from us who's already experiencing this innate state of health, it's almost like we can't help but realize our own state of well-being at the same time.

We return to that feeling that is so restful, calm and restorative — where we access our own resilience and find solutions and answers we may be looking for.

When you can give that gift to another person, it's an incredible experience for you as the listener, and it's an invaluable moment for the person being listened to. So in both directions, for both people, transformative listening is a powerful, calming and restorative experience.

Can you recall a time when you listened to someone in this way? Describe it here or on a separate piece of paper.

What You Heard in This Chapter

- When we're being listened to in this way, it really means that we're being *heard*.
- As a result of being heard, our own personal thinking quiets down, and whatever story we're telling ourselves looks less and less compelling.
- Our thinking/story doesn't connect well to another person's thinking/story, but our well-being acts like a magnet between us when even one person in the conversation realizes we're always healthy, whole, unbroken – and unbreakable.

CHAPTER 7
WE'RE TALKING ABOUT LOVE

So far, we've explored what listening traditionally looks like and also what transformative listening looks like, and then what that experience is for both the listener and the person being listened to.

In this chapter, I want to share some insights on how transformative listening can improve your relationships — and your life.

Listening in this transformative way has so much power. It has the power to make relationships that were once strained and difficult not so strained, even if only one person has an understanding of transformative listening. No matter what your relationship looks like, no matter how bad things may seem, I would encourage you to try listening to the other person in this new way. It doesn't take effort. All it really takes is an awareness of where you really are when you're listening to another person.

Are you listening to the story that either your thinking or their thinking is telling you? Or are you listening to something *beneath* the story? Is there a sense of peace within you as you're listening to them? That's how you'll know where you're listening from.

Transformative Listening Saved My Marriage

When my current husband and I were having some difficulties a few years ago — this was before I understood what I've written about here — I had a tough time listening to him except in the typical way. I was listening for information. I was looking for an opportunity to poke holes in what he was saying, and I would find myself getting defensive, angry and frustrated a lot of the time.

In other words, I wasn't hearing him at all. Things got so bad between us that we separated for a time. Looking back on it now, I can see that my inability to see through my husband's thinking, past the stories he was telling himself, to the person underneath was a big reason why we weren't getting along — and vice versa.

Eventually, we decided to get back together, and a short time later, I discovered what I'm sharing with you in this book. With this new understanding of the role of my thoughts, I began to see that my feelings weren't coming from anything my husband was or wasn't doing. For instance, if I felt angry, it became obvious to me that my husband wasn't doing anything to cause that anger; I was simply listening to, and agreeing with, momentary (key word there!) angry thinking.

As a result, my thoughts began to settle down, and I felt that inner stillness we've been talking about. From there, I began to listen to, and really hear, my husband.

Not unexpectedly, when I listened to him in a more transformative way, our relationship began to improve. I started to see my husband differently: as a person who, at times, was caught up in the world of his own thinking (just as I was), and sometimes his thinking caused him to say and do certain things that seemed like they were about me — but they weren't. Things that I used to take personally (and I mean *really* personally) no longer mattered all that much. He wasn't changing; I was.

As a simple example, I used to get really annoyed when I'd see what I called "messes" he'd leave around our home: dirty dishes in the sink, things left on the bathroom floor because he missed the garbage can, papers and bits of trash in the living room and bedroom. I began to see that he wasn't doing all of this to intentionally make me mad. First of all, my feelings were coming from momentary thoughts, not from bits of trash in the apartment (because that's impossible, of course). I knew that whatever thoughts he was having that allowed him to leave these "messes" weren't actually who he *was*.

When I could look past his thinking and my own, the feelings of connection to him, which I thought I had lost, returned — and quickly. And can you guess what happened? Over time, those "messes" began to disappear. I'm not sure how — perhaps I noticed them less often, or they really did disappear — but we both began to respond to the compassion and love I was experiencing, and both of our behavior changed.

Listening in this way, ironically, has also allowed me to talk less. There is simply less to say because there is less need for defensiveness or antagonism. If I want to talk to my husband about sharing chores, for instance, I can do it calmly and without frustration because I'm not engaging with any angry thinking I might have. In a relationship where transformative listening is central, there's more of a connection and less of a need to postulate, argue and defend a position or perspective.

Workplace Blues to Workplace Bliss?

Transformative listening isn't just for close relationships, either. I'll share an example from the workplace.

A few years ago, I was in a staff job (as opposed to a teaching job) at a university, and I felt absolutely miserable. I didn't like the work, I didn't enjoy the environment and I was starting to feel pretty desperate for an exit. The problem was, I couldn't see one. I applied for other jobs, but nothing ever panned out. I even tried starting my own business on the side, and it bombed. I felt overwhelmingly sad and stuck.

In my role at the university, I was part of weekly meetings with a small team of professionals in my department. I hated those meetings. Why? Because no one listened to each other.

Every time someone would start speaking, another person would talk over them. It looked like insanity to me, and at a certain point, I stopped talking in the meetings (and was later reprimanded for not contributing enough). I'd think to myself, "How could anyone possibly get anything accomplished in this kind of dysfunctional environment?"

One time, I asked a professor in the department, who was a communications expert, to help me figure out what was going on. He explained to me that the behavior I was witnessing was similar to "hogging the microphone." People didn't feel heard, so they attempted to grab the spotlight away from whomever was speaking. The problem, of course, is that the behavior proliferates and no one is heard except the person who can essentially yell the loudest. What to do?

Fortunately, at a time when I was feeling the most discouraged about my job, I discovered what I've been sharing with you in this book. I realized that I had a whole lot of thinking that I was listening to during those meetings, like …

"Why doesn't she let me speak? Doesn't she value me and what I have to say? I guess not!"

"What is wrong with her? Can't she see that my colleague has a good point? Let him finish!! We're never going to accomplish anything. No one listens. It's awful!"

You get the picture.

It was finally obvious to me that the source of my distress and unease wasn't what people were saying or doing, and it certainly wasn't the workplace, itself; it was the thoughts going through my head that I was giving weight to. So I decided to see what would happen if I ignored those thoughts.

The thoughts didn't go away, at least not at first. They were still there, still knocking at the door of my mind and trying to get me to respond. I simply didn't. After ignoring them for a short time, just a few days, I didn't hear them knocking quite so loudly, even when I was in the midst of one of these talking-over-each-other meetings.

The transformation was remarkable. Instead of feeling angry and frustrated, I experienced something else. I saw that my colleagues were confused about a lot of things, not the least of which was believing that if they were "hogging the microphone," they would feel better about who they were: as if their own personal power came from talking over someone else. They didn't know that security was their birthright; they didn't have to do anything in order to feel secure. Security was already within them.

Then I began noticing the pain and suffering in their eyes, and without any conscious thought, my compassion started rising like high tide, engulfing me with a strong sense of love for each one of them — something I had never experienced before with this particular group of people.

Those meetings looked less like verbal slugfests and more like opportunities for me to be in a room with amazing, talented and resourceful human beings who were simply confused about where their own security, power and well-being came from. My anger or frustration dropped away, and I found myself in awe of my colleagues' creativity and intelligence — even when they were talking over each other.

I genuinely cared about them. My relationship with them took on an entirely new hue, one that allowed me to see beyond my personal thinking — that voice in my head that's not very helpful — and into who they really were. A feeling of ease began to permeate my workdays, and I no longer felt the need to be defensive in my conversations with my teammates.

As a result, my daily stress at work disappeared, allowing me to see new career opportunities all around me. After having felt completely stuck for years, I was offered a new job (without even having to go out and get it!) and accepted it. And I did so with a clear mind and heart — not because I was desperate to escape.

It's About Love

The main reason I've written this book is because I want more people to have the experience of truly being heard. Why?

Very simply, it's about love.

Love does not exist in the intellect. Love does not exist in that chattering voice inside our heads.

Love *is* this transformative space we've been talking about: the limitless universe within us that has not one ounce of contamination but, instead, is pure, clear and whole.

Transformative listening allows you to see what is invisible and hear what is inaudible.

Because that is what is real. That's love.

To me, the way to really love someone is to connect with them from there. And what's beautiful about this listening process is that it's a natural one. There is no effort involved. All that needs to happen is seeing that you, and the other person, are not your thoughts. Those thoughts may create the momentary experience you're having — your emotions — but they are not you.

You are not the stories you hear in your head.

You are the quiet stillness that cannot be touched by the waves of feeling you experience, by your circumstances or by your thoughts.

When you listen from that stillness, and when you connect to the stillness within another person, what's experienced — on both sides — is love.

What You Heard in This Chapter

- Transformative listening can transform relationships, and quickly, because we are tapping into an infinite well of compassion and understanding.
- No matter how a relationship may look or how damaged it may appear, there is a good chance that transformative listening can improve it.
- We can hear what is inaudible, and see what is invisible – which, in the end, is love.

Chapter 8
Frequently Asked Questions

Q. Mary, I'm having a hard time believing that listening differently is going to have an impact on my relationships and my life. How is that possible? Isn't there more that I need to do to change the things in my life that I want to be better?

A. When you are able to take the two simple steps of transformative listening — ignoring the stories and thoughts in your own mind and in the other person's, and seeing past those thoughts into who both of you really are — whole new vistas will open up to you. Our "personal thinking" is extremely limited and usually not very helpful to us. When those thoughts begin to fade into the background, not only will you be able to hear other people and yourself from an entirely new perspective, your life will begin to look much richer in terms of opportunities and possibilities. The static in your head will recede, and a wave of creativity and openness will take its place. From there, anything is possible.

Q. Did you come up transformative listening all on your own, Mary?

A. Transformative listening is part of my interpretation of the insights of Sydney Banks and his expression of those insights as the Three Principles of Mind, Consciousness and Thought. Since I have personally seen how much those principles have helped me listen to myself and to others differently and truly transform my life in the process, I wanted to create a simple way for other people to experience this transformation for themselves through listening.

Q. What really makes transformative listening so different?

A. Despite the fact that it has two "steps," it is not prescriptive. It is not telling us to do anything active; in fact, it's just the opposite. It's allowing us to relax into our true selves in an effortless way, and we can do the same for the person sitting across from us simply by listening to them from this completely nonjudgmental space within us.

Q. Can transformative listening be learned by anyone?

A. Yes, because this is how we are designed to listen to each other. Our intellect, as wonderful as it is, doesn't serve a helpful purpose when it comes to relationships. Transformative listening, on the other hand, gives us a way to connect with one another from the deepest part of who we are. It's natural to experience this kind of connection, and to *want* to experience this kind of connection.

Q. Is there more for me to learn about transformative listening?

A. The principles that form the foundation of transformative listening offer endless possibilities for exploration. For me, that's the best part. The rest of my life will be an exciting journey into this beautiful feeling that's available to us in any moment.

Q. I want to learn more about the principles behind transformative listening. How do I do that?

A. I'm always available to answer questions, and I offer coaching and workshops to help you or your team solve problems with greater ease. Find me online at www.maryschiller.com or www.toloveistolisten.com. Feel free to get in touch with me: mary@maryschiller.com.

What's next? Well, it would be wonderful if you would …

Chapter 9
Share The Love

You have unique insights and discoveries every day, and I'd be absolutely thrilled to hear about them.

1) Your review of this short book on Amazon or wherever you purchased it (thank you!) would be so appreciated. Many, many thanks.

2) If this book has been valuable to you, please share it on social media, or give a copy to a friend or loved one. You might find people in your workplace, your neighborhood, your place of worship or your child's school who could benefit, too.

3) Tweet @MaryJSchiller and share an experience of transformative listening. I'd love to hear about it.

4) Subscribe online at www.toloveistolisten.com to learn more about upcoming books, classes, workshops and personalized coaching. You can also find me at www.maryschiller.com.

Thank you for reading and sharing *To Love Is To Listen: Transform Your Relationships & Your Life With A Powerful New Way To Listen*.

Much love to you,
Mary

The End ... Of Meaningless Conversations

About the Author

Mary Schiller is an author and coach who helps people experience more joy, relaxation, creativity and clarity.

She is also the author of *The Joy Formula: The simple equation that will change your life*; *Mind Yoga: The simple solution to stress that you've never heard before*; and *A-ha! How to solve any problem in record time*. More books to come, too.

Before she began coaching people and writing books, Mary was a journalist and also taught university students how to write the perfect essay. Later, she became a communications officer at an Ivy League university, and she holds advanced degrees in English and in education.

A native Californian, Mary loves the sun and the surf but also enjoys traveling. She's passionate about classical music (Beethoven is unmatched), art, photography and knitting, particularly sweaters. She's married and has a grown daughter plus two adorable cats. While Mary and her husband currently live in New York City, they may be making a move across the Atlantic very soon. Wherever she may be, you can find and connect with Mary online at www.maryschiller.com.

Printed in Poland
by Amazon Fulfillment
Poland Sp. z o.o., Wrocław